About the author

William Turner is fifty-four years old and lives in the heart of rural Cheshire with his fiancée Anoushka and their six-year-old rescue dog Tobi. His background is more of an office-based sales environment, having run his own businesses in the past. More recently he established a dog day care and training centre which inspired him to write this book and share his funny stories with any discerning dog lover. He is a qualified dog trainer and groomer, and a part time actor.

TAILS OF THE UNEXPECTED

WILLIAM TURNER

TAILS OF THE UNEXPECTED

Vanguard Press

A CIP catalogue record for this title is
available from the British Library.

ISBN 978 1 80016 251 8

*Vanguard Press is an imprint of
Pegasus Elliot MacKenzie Publishers Ltd.*
www.pegasuspublishers.com

First Published in 2022

**Vanguard Press
Sheraton House Castle Park
Cambridge England**

Printed & Bound in Great Britain

Dedication

For Ollie, always in my heart and thoughts,
much loved and missed.

Acknowledgements

With special thanks to all those who helped me over the years, including Hayleigh, Regan, Max, Joe, Jonny, Daniella, Fi and Graham.

An extra special thanks for the hugely talented illustrator, Alex.

Illustrations by: Alex Barnes-Batty
Instagram: @batty_artwork

Acknowledgements

Introduction

I will start with a little background on myself, hopefully not too much for you to want to stop reading.

My career, to say the least, has been varied and, in the words of a famous song, a roller-coaster, largely working in the sales and service industry sectors, from the travel industry, IT brokering to recruitment. I have to say I'd never particularly enjoyed any of them, at all, ever!

So, at the age of forty-something I found myself fed up and with no idea in which direction to now go. Sadly, retirement wasn't an option. I've always been a dog lover, having grown up with a furry friend by my side; in fact, I have always loved all animals and have been fascinated with nature.

An idea came to me, and with it my next cunning plan, well sort of. I had decided to build a website that would act as a blog specifically for dogs. The idea was to build up as much traffic to the site as possible in order to attract advertisers. Well at least I was taking about something I was actually genuinely interested in for the first time ever. However, this was a very slow burner and I needed an income in the meanwhile.

My girlfriend at the time suggested that I should start up a dog grooming and dog walking service in the meanwhile. Great idea, I thought, I'll do it, it sounds like lots of fun. The same night I put an ad on a well know website offering dog walking services and off I went the very next day to buy a dog van and get it kitted out with the necessary equipment.

Well, I was amazed with the response and soon found myself with a good number of dogs to walk each day. Within six months I had already become really busy and so established a dog day care centre, with training and grooming included. I had a couple of vans out on the road for collecting and dropping off dogs from their homes for day-time walking and had taken on a few extra staff. The business had expanded really quickly.

Fantastic. I also had put myself on a dog grooming course and training course, managing to graduate with flying colours.

Every dog has a different personality, training background and home lifestyle. They also by nature work as a pack. As a result, they are not always easy to control as a group. This book has been inspired by my funny experiences over the last few of years of caring for dogs. At the time none of these stories were particularly funny to me and some were actually extremely scary, after all I had the responsibly of looking after people's furry babies and I took these responsibilities very seriously. However, on reflection, these stories were hysterical afterwards.

Part 1 of this book describes each little story; all of them are true to the word.

I hope you will find them amusing and if you are a dog owner yourself, I'm sure you will be able to relate to a few of these stories.

Part 2 of this little book gives some general advice I have learned over the years, to care for your dog from the early weeks of puppyhood right through to doggy heaven. So, this section is a little more serious and hopefully creates a balanced two-part book.

Please note, no dogs or children were harmed in these stories!

PART 1

A few funny stories to start with.

CONTENTS

1. The Wolf Attack

As mentioned, I had become a qualified dog groomer at enormous expense. I had set up a little grooming parlour in the garage and was particularly proud of my efforts. It turns out this part of my new career was extremely short lived.

My first customer was Milo, a white doodle cross with a beautiful fluffy coat and a cute face to match. Until, that is, I got my shears onto poor Milo.

I had dogs to walk and needed to get Milo home with his lovely new hair cut by five p.m. I decided I would wash and dry Milo in the morning and come back to groom him later after walking some other dogs. Fine so far, he already looked and smelt like a new dog after his wash.

Walk done and dogs dropped home, I came back to start grooming Milo. It was already two-thirty p.m. by this time. I had a couple of hours, no problem, I could get this done.

Within twenty minutes of fighting and wrestling with Milo on the grooming table whist trying to shear his lovely white coat, I stood back. Oh my god, what had I done? Milo now looked like he had literally been attacked by a pack of wolves. Clumps of white hair still remained in between patches of badly, unevenly shaved parts. He looked ridiculous. I tried in vain to at least improve the total mess I had made of him. Soon four-thirty p.m. came and Milo still looked like a street dog that had been in several fights.

Panic! Thankfully I had become friendly with a local groomer so threw Milo in the van and sped around to them. Lifting Milo onto the counter I declared, "Help! He has to be home in twenty minutes and just look at the state of him. Please help!"

Milo was whisked onto the grooming table and expertly and extremely quickly sheared and clipped into some kind of half decent state. At least he no longer looked like a sheep that had been entangled in barbed wire.

I handed over some cash and drove Milo straight home, praying the owner wouldn't exclaim, "What on earth have you done to my dog?"

"Oh, doesn't he look lovely? So much better than the other groomers we took him to. Thank you so much."

Phew. I had got away with it and still made ten pounds profit on the deal!

I did actually continue to groom after this and managed to get a similar good response without having to urgently whisk dogs off to the proper professional groomer. However, my grooming equipment and table were soon to be sold on. I hated it. Back breaking, too time consuming and how to get dogs to hate you rather than love you, never ever again! Besides I much prefer the great outdoors.

So, if you're ever thinking of becoming a dog groomer, please, I implore you to think very hard about it first, it's definitely not for everyone.

2. Swimming Lesson

I try to vary my walks taking in many local parks, river walks and other natural sites of beauty we are blessed to have within a few miles of where we live.

This particular day was wet, muddy and cold. Just part of the job, you get used to it, especially living in the north west of England.

I was walking a trio from one household at a local attraction, Bramhall Hall, a lovely spot with a stately home and river running through the grounds. One of those dogs, let's call him Fido, was a particularly feisty Labrador who had the habit of running off and therefore had to be kept on the lead. He was strong, very strong, and liked to get as muddy and wet as possible.

I was walking along, Fido on the lead in one hand, brolly in the other, with Fido's two mates pitifully plodding along behind us, wishing they were home in the dry and warmth. However, Fido had other ideas. As we were walking along the riverbank, he suddenly bolted for the water, wanting to get even wetter.

This sudden turn of speed caught me unawares. As he powered towards the water, I found my feet had zero grip in the mud and I was being pulled along, still upright and feet skidding through the mud with my umbrella flapping wildly around behind me. The steep riverbank quickly approached, leaving me a choice to make in a split second: let go and risk Fido doing a runner on me or hit the deck and hang on.

It appears the latter was not the correct choice. I went down to the ground but continued to skid along in the mud, the riverbank arriving beneath me and Fido powering on towards the river with me dragging behind him, down the steep bank and headfirst, splosh, into the water with Fido barking wildly. (I actually believe he was laughing at me.)

I was completely covered in mud except for my face that had been dragged into the water first where I finally came to rest, with Fido splashing around happily in front of me.

Luckily no one had witnessed this scene but many people walked past me on the way back to the van with wry smiles on their faces.

It was very embarrassing; I must have looked like something out of *Apocalypse Now.*

3. Dive Bombing

On this occasion I was walking four dogs in a local park in Wilmslow.

It was an ordinary mild day and quiet in the park, so I was looking forward to a pleasant walk with a low chance of any unwanted incidents, or so I thought.

I love to have my dogs off lead so they can roam about, socialise and get plenty of exercise. All four dogs were doing just that. One of the dogs with me that day was called Billy, a cockerpoo. Now Billy loved to chase birds. He would dash up to them as quickly as his little legs could carry him and then, strangely, sit down with his head averted towards the sky as he watched them glide off up into the air. He never gave up chasing them or going through this exact routine, until, that is, on this day.

We were skirting the perimeter of the field hugging close to the fence. We approached some trees and everything was as normal as it should be. As I got closer to the trees with the dogs ahead of me, suddenly a chorus of barking and jumping about started. What's all this about?

There on the ground was a baby black crow flapping about. In order to protect this poor little creature, I was shooing the dogs away and trying to calm down the commotion. This proved quite successful except for the cockerpoo, Billy.

He wanted desperately to play with the baby crow that must have dropped out of his nest. Looking up into the trees I noticed for the first time Mum and Dad crow flying low and circling around the branches, until one after the other Mum and Dad swooped down towards Billy to attack.

Well, believe me, it wasn't long before Billy scampered out of the trees yelping, with the large crows still dive-bombing the poor dog in a threatening manner, but without actually harming him. Billy then sprinted full pelt towards the other dogs that had already moved on down the field, seeking refuge under the body of a large Alsatian!

The crows retreated back to their baby. Upon inspecting Billy, there was indeed no damage to him thankfully, except perhaps to his pride.

Another movie scene reminiscent of *Pearl Harbour*?

That was the day Billy gave up chasing birds.

4. The Lost Cat

I also provide home boarding to some of my dogs and its usually good fun to have a few dogs around the house.

On this occasion we had Max the spaniel, who lived with two cats. The owners were going on holiday and asked if I would look after Max and one of the cats too, Marley. The other cat was fine to be left at the clients' home as he was an outdoor type of cat and the neighbours would pop over to put more food down for him.

Well, I hadn't signed up to this and wondered if my Ollie would particularly appreciate a cat being round the house too. Ollie is an extremely good natured and obedient dog and I though it shouldn't be a problem and agreed to take the cat in as well. As it turned out it wasn't Ollie that would be the problem but the cat itself. He was a house cat who was really quite timid and shy.

On collecting Max and his buddy I thought it best to put Marley in the dining room to get it used to his new surroundings and to make sure Ollie could be introduced to him slowly. Max settled in and was playing in the garden with Ollie so I went to go and release Marley to let him have a wander around the house. I entered the dining room to find Marley… no Marley! I searched and searched the dining room thinking he would have climbed up onto the shelves to find a safe spot but just couldn't find him anywhere.

I called Jo, my girlfriend, to come and help me with the search but neither of us could find Marley anywhere. Did Marley shoot passed me when I put him in there? Had he bolted between my legs without me noticing and run off into the garden? Had he therefore escaped? He was just gone. Poof, vanished, absolutely nowhere to be seen. Oh no, what on earth would the owners think? Should I call them? They were about to board a plane to some exotic destination. I couldn't just ruin their holiday. The search continued.

Nothing. Half an hour had passed and Marley was, it seemed, possibly lost forever. I then had an obscure thought and went to fetch a torch. Clicking the torch on I shone it up the chimney. There in the darkness two little eyes brightly lit up under the torch's beam. Marley had climbed up the chimney! Well at least he was safe. However, the cat was quite a long way up and out of my reach.

"Here, kitty."

Cat treats, comforting words, etcetera… no good. Marley wasn't budging. The broom came out and was stuck up the chimney to try to knock him back down. Well, it worked. Marley came tumbling down with an enormous black cloud of soot which after landing in the fireplace spread out across the dining room with a coughing Marley spitting soot and snarling at me with hatred.

Marley was banished from the dining room and spent the next few days on the back of the sofa in the lounge where there was a fake fireplace. Ollie occasionally went to give Marley a sniff to find a swishing paw with claws retracted digging into his nose.

Ollie left Marley alone, Marley stayed in the lounge and all was well, except, that is, for the constant mushroom of soot raising out of Marley's coat every time he had a little scratch.

5. 'Tight' Squeeze

One of the less pleasant sides of the job is dealing with huge amounts of poo on a daily basis.

Poo is not my favourite thing in the world, and recounting this story always makes me feel quite queasy, to be honest.

On this particular walk the poo quantities were as expected, except for one Labrador who had an issue with something he must have eaten. Bailey was a fine specimen of a lab and a big fella, even for this breed's standard.

I had taken on part time staff over the busy periods and had with me a lovely young lady called Regan who is the daughter of some friends.

So, Bailey was walking along and squatted in the appropriate position to do his business. Upon wondering over to bag up the deposit he kindly left for me, I noticed there was still a little something left dangling from his rear end which was obviously causing him some distress.

Being the kind and loving dog carer that I am, it seemed further inspection was necessary to help him out. I reached Bailey and approached him from behind, gently lifting his tail to inspect his discomfort. Indeed, there was something still dangling. I grabbed another poo bag and, averting my head, I got hold the offending object to remove it. Upon pulling the object for what I thought would be a quick release and job done, it appeared this wasn't going to be as straight forward as I hoped.

The dangly object kept coming, I kept pulling. Pulling and pulling. The object just kept coming from Bailey's posterior. I was becoming quite distressed by now; Bailey was in the meanwhile wagging his tail tenfold, obviously enjoying the sensation of me removing the item causing him discomfort. Seconds had passed and I was still pulling. At this point with my averted head, I caught a glimpse of my co-walker, Regan. She by now was literally rolling around on the floor crying with laughter as I kept pulling. It seemed that a minute had passed before the pulling stopped, but I'm sure it was probably only about ten seconds.

Bailey, now totally satisfied, walked on, leaving me to deal with what must have once been some kind of garment. A pair of tights maybe?

I think I did him a good service that day and saved him a trip to the vets; it could easily have blocked his intestines had it remained in his belly.

Not my most pleasant experience it has to be said!

6. School Outing

I have a few stories of a similar nature relating to this, but I think this was the funniest of them (afterwards, anyway).

Another day, quite recently, another nice walk this time along a lovely popular lakeside spot. Today I was with the amazing Graham who now works with me full time. Four dogs each, so eight dogs in total. I'm not one for walking dogs on leads at all, I love to see them all running free, enjoying each other's company and effectively having a little party. Some dogs, yes, I need to keep on leads as they can be a flight threat. But today was good, all eight dogs off lead.

Parked up, Graham and I got all the dogs out of the van.

Among the eight was a very bouncy, inquisitive and perhaps over friendly puppy cockerpoo, named Hugo. Immediately as we entered the lakeside compound there happened to be a circle of about a dozen small children all sitting down with three adults, probably out on a nature trip school outing or similar. Hugo was extremely excited and spotted this circle immediately. He charged over towards the children. As I mentioned, lead walking is not my thing, the problem being on this day Hugo was swiftly followed by another seven dogs happy to be released from the van cages.

I kid you not, total and utter carnage followed within a second. Hugo arrived first at the circle of kids, to be greeted with a couple of giggles and some shouting until the other seven dogs also descended into the circle. All the dogs were jumping up, licking, barking and rummaging through school bags in a mad frenzy of screaming and crying children who must have felt like they were in some nightmare story of the hounds of Baskerville. The adult supervisors were, of course, in total panic too as the dogs charged from child to child, some of whom were now fleeing off in all directions.

Graham and I probably didn't help by charging into the circle to try and calm the scene down and gather the excited dogs away from the children. We actually in fairness manged to achieve this fairly quickly and moved away from the carnage with the dogs, almost as quickly as it had started. A couple of the adults were shouting incoherent abuse at us whilst the other adult was running after the fleeing children.

We disappeared from the scene as quickly as possible with the eight happy dogs who had just enjoyed the encounter far more than the children. Graham had, during these few seconds, noticed a couple of ladies who were chatting on one of the park benches that overlooked the scene. Apparently one of these ladies had almost slid off the bench due to laughing so much.

They both clearly realised there was no actual danger to the children. Well, I think we made their day anyway.

Graham and I did an extended walk that morning in the hope the group of children had departed and there were no police waiting to question us.

I would like to stress no harm was done during this episode to the dogs or the children. I have to say we did have a giggle about it later that day but at the time it wasn't as funny as the two ladies clearly thought.

7. Picnic Anyone?

This story kind of follows on from the previous one, and was always inevitable really. I'm actually surprised it took almost a year of dog walking to happen first time; it's happened several times since and certainly will again. It's probably a story many of you dog owners can relate to.

But for my first effort, it was the worst (or best, depending on your viewpoint).

People love to picnic. Sun's out, let's hit the park with our old moth-eaten tartan blanket, get out the cool bag and buy all the sausage rolls and pork pies left on the shop shelves. And perhaps a beer or two.

Stupidly I'd never really given too much thought about this being a potential problem. This day I was on my own with three Labs and another smaller dog, a Shitzu. I'm really not picking on Labs, honest, and I only have about five on my books, but they do like their food.

Usual scene, got the dogs out of the van and into the park where they could be released from their leads to run free and have fun.

Beyond the gate sat a group of four young ladies, sitting around the beautifully laid out spread of food and drinks. The attack was immediate. One Lab caught the scent and charged towards the young (what I assumed were) students, followed in a line of attack by the other two Labs and lastly the Shitzu who was simply chasing the rest in pure excitement.

Food scattered, drinks flew in the air, dogs were barking and wildly going from food container to food container, girls were screaming and shouting, and the Shitzu was just causing further chaos by jumping all over the girls. It was like a war zone where a hand grenade had just exploded. And there was absolutely nothing I could do to control the situation.

This rampage went on for what felt like several minutes but may have only been one, but within that time everything within the students' lovely picnic was either eaten, trodden in, knocked over or was spread all over the girls' clothes. I really didn't quite know what to do. When I had finally shooed the dogs away, all I could think was to offer some financial compensation to the girls, who were in fairness now laughing about the whole situation.

I quickly reached into my back pocket and thrust what I think was about £30 into one of the girl's hands and scarpered quickly whilst shouting my apologies over my shoulder.

Well, I never dared to look back behind me but just kept walking quickly away with three very fulfilled Labs and one very happy Shitzu who seemed to have enjoyed the screaming as much as anything.

Never did I set foot in that park again. I would have died with embarrassment if I ever saw those poor girls again.

8. The 18th Green

One of my regular walks is along the Mersey River. A lovely walk especially for those dogs, like my Ollie, who love to swim or play in the water.

On this stretch of the river there is a golf course on either side.

Now I apologise to all golfers but it's just not my thing. In fact, I actually just don't get it. My idea of taking part in sport is for enjoyment first, and winning second. Golf is the most unenjoyable sport I have ever participated in; it's slow, serious, stupidly complex and rather silly. The rule book is like *War and Peace* and *Encyclopaedia Britannica* rolled into one.

Well, I doubt they have a rule for what happened this day.

The riverbank walk has a path on two levels. This day I took the higher level whereby you can overlook the golf course.

People were doing their thing on the course, lining up their shots, waggling their bottoms, holding up their putters to apparently show the undulations of the green and generally faffing about whilst studying their scorecards.

We approached a green and I stood to watch, partly out of faint interest and partly to put off the serious looking fella who was pulling out his putter from the enormous golf bag. This chap was taking forever, pacing up and down the green, crouching on his knees to line up his putt. Finally, he was hovering over his little white ball getting ready to attempt to plop it into a hole in a field.

From the corner of my eye, I spotted Daisy the collie charging down the embankment towards the green. Oh no, I thought, this is going to be trouble. Daisy was rushing towards the golfer who had now stood up straight. I really thought Daisy was going to grab the golf ball and run off, which would have been rather funny to me in honesty.

In fact, Daisy did one better, rushing towards the serious looking chap and in the process of greeting him, she actually kicked his golf ball which then proceeded to roll off the green at some pace. Worse, his golf ball rolled so fast off the green it in fact managed to find its way into a greenside bunker. I kid you not, this guy went absolutely completely berserk.

I simply looked at him, called Daisy to come back to me, and kept walking with Mr Long Socks continuing to scream abuse at me. What he couldn't see was the wide grin on my face as I walked off, not saying a word to him.

Well done, Daisy, I really enjoyed that.

Sorry again to all golfers, each to their own, I say!

9. A Winter's Day

As I mentioned we also do home boarding. It's lovely having a few dogs in the house lounging next to you on the sofa on a quiet evening just watching TV.

It was a winter morning and I still wasn't showered or dressed yet. Cue the doorbell.

I think most of our dogs start barking when the doorbell sounds, my Ollie is no exception. On this occasion I had Reggie staying with me. Reggie is a Shar Pei. I lot of people consider Shar Peis either an ugly or scary breed of dog. I beg to differ. Reggie to me is both beautiful and really sweet. He was one of my first ever clients and I had developed a strong bond with him. However, Reggie was exceptionally strong.

I went to the front door followed by Reggie, barking loudly, and shouted, "Who is it?"

"Delivery, mate," came the answer.

"Okay, do I need to sign?"

"No, mate."

"Okay, just leave it on the doorstep, please."

"Okay, mate."

There was a lead on the hallway table, so I thought I would hook Reggie up to stop him doing a runner and open the door to retrieve the package.

At this point I should note I was wearing nothing but my underpants. I opened the door; Reggie darted out dragging me with him. Rather unfortunately my trailing foot caught the door, slamming it shut behind me and I had somehow in addition dropped the lead which also got trapped in the shut door.

So, there I was in the cold, wearing nothing but pants, with a barking Reggie trapped by his lead outside with me. Understandably as I was practically naked, I didn't of course have any keys on me. In the meanwhile, Reggie's barking was attracting the attention of those climbing into their cars to embark on the journey to work.

It was embarrassing to say the least. I timidly crossed the road trying to hide my modesty to our neighbours who had a house key, rang the bell... no answer. Lots of people were by now watching, giggling and no doubt I had made their day for a little story to tell when they had finished their commute.

In a now high state of blushing cheeks (whilst my other cheeks were beginning to freeze!) I crossed back over the road, Reggie still barking, trapped in the front door, and entered the back gate to our garden.

Thank the lords the back gate and back door were both open, my embarrassment over and Reggie now retrieved from his trapped position.

Not the start to the day I was looking for.

10. Head Lock

This was without doubt the scariest moment I have had to date.

We frequently looked after a pure white toy poodle called Charlie. In this case I'm using his real name as he emigrated to Australia and I would be surprised to say the least if this little book hit the paperback shelves in Sydney any time soon.

Charlie was lovely, I mean really lovely. He was so sweet and cuddly and had bags and bags of character. He would run along and play with the biggest of dogs, keeping up with them no problem. We looked after him all day every day and in fact at one point he stayed with us for three months solid whilst his family were in Australia sorting out houses and jobs before moving. We became extremely fond of little Charlie.

It was an ordinary day with a number of day care dogs collected and walked, now deposited in the garden to roam around and play. Little Charlie seemed particularly excited that morning and was charging around the garden at high speed in big circles. (Boy, he could shift for such a little fella.) One of the other dogs was quietly standing watching Charlie's solo performance.

Once Charlie had finished his mad frenzy and finally exhausted himself, the other much larger dog who had been observing him, casually wandered over to him, in a completely non-threatening way, and picked him up in his enormous jaw... by the head! Charlie froze, I froze, and the big dog walked on calmly with Charlie's little back legs dangling from his mouth. I came to my senses after the initial shock of what I was seeing and sprinted over towards them, screaming the other dog's name and shouting 'drop' at the top of my voice.

By the time I had reached them, the other dog had turned around to face me and gently placed Charlie back down on the ground, who was then looking up at that big jaw and wagging his tail again.

He was completely unharmed, thank goodness, just a little soggy in dog's saliva. I'd never seen anything like it. I suppose looking back it was rather like a lion picking up its cub, but of course that is usually by the scruff of the neck and not actually by its head.

But my goodness, I was completely terrified at the time.

11. Give Us a Kiss

One of the walks I frequently used was a lovely big park which was partly a nature reserve and partly farm land.

There are proper paths that go off in different directions and loop around the outskirts of a fenced piece of farm land that held cows and bulls. I was always on high alert when taking this path as on a couple of occasions one or two of the dogs had got through the fence and taken an interest in those extremely large and frankly scary bulls, but luckily, I had never had a serious situation in these circumstance as the dogs had returned back through the fence to the path when called.

This day, however, was very different indeed. I had the usual four dogs with me on the late afternoon walk and was rounding a corner of the path and enjoying myself watching the dogs run and play. The corner was like a right angle so you couldn't see what was coming until meeting the top of the corner. I looked ahead once I had navigated the bend and stopped dead. There were not one, but two, massive bulls on the path just one hundred yards ahead, obviously having somehow escaped from the fenced field.

The dogs spotted them at once too, and three of them had stopped dead with me, looking rather apprehensive of what lay ahead. The fourth dog, Maloo, however, didn't seem at all concerned and started running towards the two huge and muscular bulls. There was nothing I could do, it was too late, he had reached the bulls already. I tried shouting, but literally nothing came out of my mouth like I had had some kind of seizure or something. I didn't want to carry on as I was in fear of the other dogs' lives as well as my own; in fact, I think I had started to take a few steps backwards. I just watched in horror.

Maloo wandered right up to the nearest of the bulls. The bull was remaining still, and bent its head down towards Maloo who sniffed the bull's mouth, then give it a big lick. The bull responded. It gave him an even bigger great big lick back. Maloo then turned around to face me and the other dogs, wagging his tail as if to say, "Hey, I like this big funny looking doggie." I had found my voice again and quietly called, "Maloo, come, boy."

He responded and trotted back towards me. The rear bull remained still. The nearer one, that Maloo had just kissed, began to amble towards us. Maloo had reached me by then, so I just turned and ran as fast as I could without looking back, all four dogs following me woofing like it was some kind of a game.

Every time I think back to this instance, I still feel absolute shock as to what had happened, and complete amazement that nothing far more sinister had occurred.

I know it sounds like I'm making this up, but it wasn't some weird dream, it really did happen.

12. Bath Time

Whilst I was still doing the grooming in the earlier days, I had a call from a potential new client. She had a dog called Freddy, a bulldog, who had a bad skin condition and needed regular washing in a special medicated shampoo once a week. The client had become a little too old to be able to handle this weekly task.

After agreeing it was no problem, yes, I could do that, I arranged to go and meet Freddy and his owner the next day. On approaching the new client's door, she opened it whilst I was still only halfway up her path, obviously waiting for me. Freddy also popped out too in order to see what was going on and say hello. Well, he was enormous, a mean like the biggest dog I had ever seen. He was lovely and friendly and greeted me like an old pal. Anyway, we filled out some appropriate paperwork and agreed for me to come back in a couple of days to collect Freddy for his medical wash.

The situation at home was that we had a wet room in the basement where there was a utility room as well. However, the staircase down was quite narrow and steep, so I was immediately wondering if it might be difficult to get Freddy down to the wet room.

The time came for me to go and collect Freddy. Getting him in the van proved rather difficult to begin with. It was not only his size, but he was very unfit and slow in his movements, and incredibly heavy, so I was unable to pick him up. Eventually after lots of pushing and shoving I got Freddy into the van and headed home, armed with a special bottle of shampoo and full instructions of how much to apply, etcetera.

Freddy got out of the van easily enough, and up the small three steps to the front door and into the house. The utility room in the basement was off the kitchen. I still had him on the lead and opened the basement door leading to the steep narrow staircase. I went first, gently tugging Freddy and encouraging him to follow me. I was down a few of the steps now as he approached the top. He stuck his head through the door, took one look, and began to tug me back. I held firm and kept calmingly talking to him to get him to join me down the steps. He wasn't having it, so I had to tug a little harder. Freddy had planted his front paws firmly on either side of the doorway and was not willing to move. After much persuasion, pulling and grabbing his paws to release them from the doorway, I eventually got him through the entrance and down a couple to steps. So, he gave in and very slowly and carefully wandered down the narrow stairs.

Washing him wasn't such a problem, and after two applications of the shampoo and a quick dry I was satisfied that a good job had been done. Now to get him back upstairs, dried off properly and back home. Well, I thought getting him downstairs was difficult enough, and it hadn't really crossed my mind that going the reverse way was also going to be a problem... wrong!

Freddy wouldn't follow me back up, even on lead. He was proving too strong for me and just wouldn't have it. It had already been two hours since I collected him, and I had promised him back in an hour and a half. Twenty more minutes later we were still in the basement. Then an idea hit me. If I got behind him, I could maybe push him back up the stairs. This happily, eventually worked. However, it took another twenty minutes as I had to shoulder barge him up step by step, my feet slipping all the time on the wet tiled floor behind me.

I did see Freddy again, but he had to put up with a cold hosepipe shower outside from then on.

13. Play Time

One day I was doing the rounds, collecting some dogs for a walk. It was about three p.m. and the roads were quite busy with all the mums and dads doing the school run to collect their little precious bundles of joy.

I was collecting the last dog in a cul-de-sac that had bollards at the end of the road to stop two-way traffic. Across the main road from the bollards was an infant school. I pulled up, jumped out of the van and pulled the sliding side door open, heading towards the house to collect Bruno the Lab. I got the front door open and Bruno jumped up at me in his usual excited greeting. With Bruno I never had to worry, he would rush to the van and jump into the space between the front seats and the cages in the back.

However, in doing so he must have caught his collar in one of the latches of a lower cage, thus letting Frieda the Irish terrier escape from said cage. So, Bruno jumped in and Frieda jumped out. She darted to the end of the cul-de-sac, dashed across the busy main road that was coming and going with parents' cars and sprinted into the children's playground, with me hot on her heels.

Forgetting in my haste to slide the van side door closed, I was followed by Bruno, who had decided to join in the game and ran after me, across the road and into the playground.

Some children were screaming for joy at the sight of two dogs entering their territory, however others were screaming in fear. This of course resulted in both dogs getting even more excited, with Bruno jumping up to children and knocking them to the floor, whilst Frieda was charging around and around the playground, darting in and out of the children's legs.

All hell had broken loose in a matter of seconds; kids were running for their lives, angry parents were shouting and waving their fists at me whilst picking up their children from the floor and trying to comfort them, and teachers were busy trying to catch the dogs to stop the chaos. I managed to grab Bruno by the collar, but Frieda was unstoppable in using all her speed and agility to refrain from being caught.

Eventually one of the parents managed to grab her, so I got her by the collar and frog marched them both back across the road and into the van.

I headed back to the playground, head hanging in shame, and did my best to apologise.

Luckily no one was hurt, but I quite rightly got a good verbal ear bashing from some of the parents, whilst others were now smiling about it.

I jumped into the van and sped off without looking back.

14. Swanning About

This story involves my own dog, Ollie. Of course, I'm totally biased, but Ollie is an extremely clever, good-natured dog who adores people so much (more than other dogs actually), loves his twice daily walks and adores swimming.

I always wanted a dog that would swim properly, rather than just paddle around. So, when he was still a very young pup, one summer's day I took him to a local water park with a big lake, carried him into the water and eased him in for his first swimming lesson. Ever since he has wanted to go into water at every opportunity, he can't get enough, even in the winter.

This water park is a beautiful spot, with lots of wildlife, especially ducks, geese and swans. It's very popular with walkers, cyclists and joggers. The perimeter of the lake is exactly one mile, so joggers like it especially so they can count their laps and therefore miles. Ollie loves it for the swimming opportunity and I love it for the ice cream van in the car park.

Anyway, we were walking around the lake and stopping every once in a while, so I could throw a ball into the lake for him to swim out to and retrieve. There are a few ramps around the lake that go down to the water and a few little wooden jetties on the water's edge for fishermen to use. As I threw the tennis ball out into the water again for Ollie, it landed a little close to this rather beautiful, majestic and proud looking swan.

Ollie dived into the water in pursuit of his tennis ball, swimming with a perfect wake forming behind him. Ollie would never harm another animal and didn't bother with chasing any birds (only squirrels), but he looked as if he was homing in on the swan. As he got close to the tennis ball the swan obviously decided it was under threat from Ollie, and so defended itself, by attacking.

It squawked a warning at Ollie, who didn't retreat as he was so focused on his tennis ball, and then pounce... the swan's head went thumping down towards Ollie, and what looked like with massive force struck the water right next to Ollie's nose.

Now I've heard an urban myth that a swan could break a man's arm with its beak so I was obviously terrified the swan would go in for a further attack on Ollie. He did give a startled, gargled yelp, grabbed the tennis ball, and headed for shore.

It seemed no harm was done to Ollie as the swan thankfully hadn't made a direct hit, but had only connected with the water in front of his nose. Ollie came running between my legs (as he does when he's scared) and I gave him a comforting cuddle. He has never gone near a swan again and I'm glad to say it didn't put him off swimming.

15.Three in a Bed

An additional service I provided for my dog clients, on a more limited scale, was home boarding.

Dog owners these days in general allow their dogs into their home, and more often than not on their rugs, carpets, sofas and even beds. Not like a generation before who often kept their dogs in an outside kennel at night, or perhaps just the kitchen or utility area.

Ollie has certainly never been in a kennel, and never will be. I just don't like the idea of them at all.

Consequently, we had pretty relaxed dog rules, not just for Ollie, but also for our overnight guests. On this occasion we had Hattie the Dalmatian and yet another Lab called Jack. Now no offense intended to the rather beautiful Hattie, but she was a large girl. When I say large, she was by far the biggest Dalmatian I have ever seen. Unfortunately, she had a few health problems and poor joints, so her main interest in life was food, and consequently she was rather overweight. Jack was a normal sized black Lab, so not small anyway.

When we had doggie guests staying in the house, I would sleep in the spare bedroom, that had a single bed in it. On these occasions our Ollie would usually choose to sleep in the spare room with me, normally just on the floor but at times throughout the night he might choose to join me and jump onto the bed.

News at ten watched, a quick wander in the garden with the dogs to avoid any accidents during the night and it was time for bed. Both Hattie and Jack had stayed before and so were used to being invited upstairs at bedtime. So up we all went.

After the usual night time routine I climbed into the single bed. Ollie followed and settled down on the floor with Hattie and Jack standing in the doorway, wondering what to do with themselves. Jack made his move first and sheepishly entered the small room, and jumped onto the bed with me. I shifted over as much as I could to give him room and because I didn't want him on top of me.

Hattie had observed this from the doorway and decided it wouldn't be fair for her to sleep on the landing alone, despite the comfy dog bed that was provided, and she took a great leap and landed firmly on top of me. I have always been happy to share my bed with Ollie, but this was taking it a little far. I tried to move Hattie off me, but any spare space had already been taken by Jack. I was pinned down by her weight and bulk, unable to move.

That was how I spent the whole night. Hattie kicking her legs out in dream land, lying on top of me, and Jack with his face next to my ear, snoring loudly.

Needless to say, I got very little sleep that night and I had to adjust the sleeping arrangements the following night.

All part of the service.

16.The Walk's Not Over

This was one of my first ever walks, not long after the business had got going.

Consequently, I only had Ollie and one other dog with me, a fun filled and highly energetic cocker spaniel named Sandy. Sandy was great fun and Ollie really liked him too. They would sprint ahead on the walks alongside each other, both of them absolutely flat out, wagging and barking encouragement at each other. It was really lovely to watch them enjoy the other's company and expel all that excess energy. Both Ollie and Sandy were great swimmers too, so a river walk seemed the most appropriate for doggie fun value.

The walk was coming to a close and the three of us were heading back towards the van, still hugging the riverbed. Sandy, I think, had deliberately slowed down, sensing the walk was nearly over. As we approached the car park Ollie obediently went to the front door (he gets to sit up front with me) and I opened the door and in he hopped, settling onto the provided towel on the front seat. Sandy however had other ideas.

He was standing back, about thirty metres from the van, just looking at me.

"Come on, Sandy, time to go home." No reaction. I walked towards him with his lead in hand, and got to within a couple of feet. Sandy back-pedalled.

"Sandy, come here." Nothing. I approached him again to grab his collar and hook him on the lead to guide him towards the van door. He back-pedalled again.

"Sandy, come on." He moved further away. I walked quickly towards him and he turned and fled back towards the river. I call Ollie (the door was still open) and he jumped out and followed me back towards the river in search of Sandy.

Sandy was back in the water, happily swimming around. Well, I could hardly wade in and get him, so I just kept calling his name. Ollie was barking at him from the riverbank. Eventually Sandy came to shore and again I tried to grab him, but he was just too quick. He sprinted back towards the car park. Well, I thought, at least he is heading in the right direction. Ollie back in the van, I tried again to get Sandy. He just wouldn't have it, and I was beginning to get frustrated so raised my voice at him but his stubbornness persisted.

To worsen my frustration a small crowd had gathered to watch. It was becoming embarrassing now too. Then a fellow dog walker came along who I knew. She joined me in trying to catch Sandy. No joy, he just flatly refused to let us close enough to grab him. Over half an hour had passed now and I needed to get on with my next walk. Another fifteen minutes later, still no luck, my fellow dog walker had moved on to get on with her day, and so had the crowd.

I was left with one choice. I rang the owner. He thankfully understood and raced out of work to assist me. It actually took him another fifteen minutes to get Sandy on his lead and back into the van. The whole episode had taken almost an hour and a half.

As time went on in the job, I had other dogs who also liked to play 'catch me if you can' at the end of a walk but I got to know the dogs individually better by then and knew to hook them up on their leads five minutes before the end of a walk.

Part 2

This section of the book is a little more serious, so pay attention! It covers everything I have learnt about the general health and welfare of caring for a dog. It's a lifelong commitment and so the key is to know what to expect. I want to share with you the knowledge I have learnt over the years. It doesn't, of course, cover every single aspect of being a dog owner, but is a good general guideline.

From puppy…

…to doggy heaven.

1. Choosing Your Puppy

Research, research, research.

This is so important. You need to consider your lifestyle, house size (garden or not), family situation, work situation, how much spare time you have, how much spare time other people in your household have, your finances (it's not that cheap to keep a dog for life) and be as prepared as you can before the arrival of your new pup.

There are so many breeds out there, so I couldn't go through them all, but they all have different needs, space requirements, food, exercise, etcetera. Don't just assume that a little dog needs less exercise and would be happy to sit on your lap all day, it's not the case.

If you decide to get a dog from a dog home, great, I'm all for it, but the same principles apply. Don't just get the first dog that looks you in the eye and wags his tail, saying, 'please take me home with you'. I know it's difficult not to, but you must be sensible. I have done some charity fund raising for Battersea Dogs and Cats Home and I have been to visit a more local dogs' home. It's absolutely heart breaking seeing all those dogs that need a good home and I struggled not to take half a dozen home with me.

If you have decided to get a puppy from a breeder, that's okay too. However, please also research the breeder themselves... are they licensed, is it just some awful puppy farm, have the dogs had initial vaccinations, have they been microchipped? If the breeder hasn't done these basic things already, then I would avoid them. Some people are just in it for the money (with some breeds fetching well over £1000 these days) and they have no regard for the welfare of the dog. They should be asking about you to make sure the puppy is going into the right home and environment. If again they just want the money and don't have any questions about yourself, then I would just avoid these types of breeders.

So please consider all the facts of your lifestyle and research the right breed to suit your needs. There is so much information on the Internet on every single breed going and how much exercise, training and so on they all need.

This little dog should be with you for life, so don't just get one on a whim. Consider everything very hard first.

2. Preparation

Once you have made the correct decision on which breed you are going to get, and from where, there is plenty of preparation work you need to do in advance of collecting your puppy.

First you need to choose a name. Now it doesn't really matter what you call your new puppy, but two pieces of advice here. First use a name preferably with just one or maximum two syllables. Whilst some dogs, it is believed, can learn up to five hundred words, long words are harder for them to understand, hence use a short name for them. Secondly, stick with the name. Don't be persuaded to change your puppy's name a couple of weeks down the line, even if your children beg you to. Discuss a name first, decide on it and stick to it for life.

Secondly, go shopping! I would always recommend getting a suitably sized cage/crate and make a good space in the house to put it. We will come onto cage/toilet training later. In addition, you will need to get a dog bed, blankets (old ones knocking about your house are fine), toys, lead and collar with a couple of dog tags with your name, telephone number (always good to have a spare), water and feeding bowls, puppy training pads (lots and lots of them!) and of course food. We will go into more detail on nutrition again later.

Also, if you're planning on using a dog walker or dog day care centre, research them. Speak to a few and meet up with them. Make sure they have insurance and are registered with the council. There are too many unprofessional dog carers out there who are only in it for easy money. I have heard about some who will pick the dogs up, shove them in a car and drive them around for a bit, or worse, sit in a car park having a smoke with the dogs in the back, and then let them out for five minutes before taking them home again, rather than actually giving your dog the necessary exercise and socialisation that they require. Check them out properly.

Now you're more or less ready to collect your new puppy, but see the next chapter for other things you need to consider as well.

3. Welfare Considerations

There are a number of other considerations to think about once you have welcomed your new puppy home.

Vaccinations

Your breeder (or dogs' home) should have completed the initial vaccinations that every puppy needs to protect it from all the nasty diseases that could affect your dog's long-term welfare. Please make sure you have asked them about this already. You need to be aware of what further vaccinations your puppy will need before he is allowed out into the big wide world. Your puppy cannot go for walks before he has had the twelve-week vaccinations necessary. Ask your vet.

Vet

Talking of vets, make sure you register your new dog with a good, reputable local vets as he will need further vaccinations and ongoing care. Your dog will require annual boosters, flea and worm treatment and regular health checks. I would recommend getting an additional specialised flea and tick collar too. There not cheap but generally last around six months so it is well worth the investment.

Microchipping

Make sure your new pup has been microchipped, and get this registered at the vets of your choice. Also make sure you have got at least two dog tags made. Only put your name and telephone number on and *not* the dog's name. I say this because sadly people do steal dogs and if they can see the dog's name on the tag, they will use it and it could encourage your dog to go with them.

Insurance

I would definitely recommend taking out dog insurance. Again, there are many companies out there offering this service, so all I can recommend is research it. Check out what cover they offer, including for any ongoing repeat treatment, operations, etcetera, etcetera.

Neutering

Unless you are planning on breeding, I would always recommend getting your dog neutered. This usually can't be done until after six months. You never know what they may be getting up to behind a tree in a park, and before you know it you may notice a swelling tummy in your bitch or your male dog doing what is a natural instinct to him! There are enough homeless dogs in this country without your own dog adding to the numbers. In addition, if you are planning on using a dog walker or day care centre, they should insist on your dog being neutered anyway before allowing them into the fold.

Grooming

Regular grooming is necessary for many breeds. Please make sure that you again research this and make sure your dog is getting groomed as much as the breed needs. Besides the dog's comfort, it will be easy to keep them cleaner. If a dog gets badly matted, it will eventually cause a great deal of pain and poor skin conditions because the matts will eventually twist the dog's skin, creating sores. In order to help prevent this, brush your dog at least three times a week if you can. It will also help them to be less anxious when going to the groomers.

In addition, your dog's claws will need regular clipping. Unfortunately, a lot of groomers forget to do this, so give them a reminder. Some breeds also have what are called dewclaws. These are found higher up a dog's front legs and don't get naturally worn down as they are not in contact with the ground. As a result, these claws often grow longer and in some cases I have seen them get so long that they grow back into the dog's legs, very painful of course for them. So watch out for these too.

4. Eight to Twelve Weeks

This for me is without doubt the most important period of development of your puppy, closely followed by twelve weeks to six months in the next chapter.

During this period your puppy won't be allowed to go on walks yet as the full vaccinations won't yet have been completed. However, there is plenty you can teach him at home.

I would always recommend a cage or pen area for your puppy, better still both. Hopefully you have done your preparation and have already set up an area in your house for this, with nice bedding, water bowl, a few toys and puppy pads either within the pen or directly outside the cage. This space will become your puppy's go to area of safety and comfort for him. A dog is very unlikely to have an accident in his bed or cage, so will hopefully automatically start to do his business on the puppy pads. Always encourage your pup when he uses the puppy pads. This will be your puppy's sleeping area, so when he gets tired and is ready for a nap, pop him in the cage or pen so he gets used to it.

If you have a garden, it should be safe to let your puppy outside in this area only (so long as there are no signs of foxes in your garden as your pup could pick up an infection from that). Don't be tempted to go on any proper walks yet. Therefore, again praise and reinforce him with a treat every time he goes to the loo outside.

At this stage I would also put a collar on your puppy. Make sure it's not too tight and check it regularly as your puppy will grow quickly. Allow two fingers on top of each other as a marker for the collar tightness. In other words, make sure you can fit two fingers under the collar and his neck. A trick that many people miss out on is to also (a couple of times a day) attach the lead onto the collar and let your puppy drag it around the house (supervised of course) so he gets used to the feel of everything.

Talk to your dog. It's not silly. Your pup will start to understand words you need him to learn (good boy, wee wee, sit, come, dinner, etcetera). Always encourage and praise your dog and reinforce good behaviour in this way. You can definitely also reinforce good behaviour not just with praise but also with a little treat. Say 'good boy' and then back it up with a small treat. Your dog will learn very quickly how he can win your praise and a little treat. Repetition is the key. Never shout at your dog or smack him for bad behaviour, he will only get scared and pee on your carpet! You can say 'no' in a sterner voice, sure no problem. Training should always be positive. Make it into a game.

During these first four weeks of having your puppy at home, everyone in the household should be building a positive relationship with your dog, that should last a lifetime.

Other little tips you should work on during this period, that again people may not realise they should do. Start to brush your pup, he needs to get used to it so now is the perfect time to start. Also (it sounds daft), but take him for a drive in the car. Dogs can be prone to car sickness so again this should help to get your puppy used to this feeling. Lastly, although you cannot take your pup for a walk yet, take him out with you, but carry him in your arms.

Go down the high street, he will be amazed at everything he sees. It will get him used to the noise, other people who will stop and want to stroke your new pup, seeing other dogs on leads, cars, buses, cyclists, etcetera, etcetera. These are all brand new sites to your puppy. He will learn from it and will hopefully not fear all the hustle and bustle of human life when it comes to going on proper walks.

Keep up with the toilet training, remembering positive reinforcement only.

5. Twelve Weeks to Six Months (and Onwards)

This period is equally important for your pup. He should have completed all the necessary vaccinations by now and be allowed out on his first proper walk, how exciting!

First of all, I would recommend short walks only as your pup is still growing and a long hike at this stage could affect his bone and joint development. Twenty minutes two to three times a day is fine. Your pup will get tired, so put him in his safe pen area when he wants to sleep.

Obviously, recall isn't that good by now, so keep him on lead too. All the new sights and sounds in your local park, plus seeing much bigger dogs, cyclists, etcetera could freak him out and before you know it, he has fled towards the park entrance and across the road. However, please let him socialise with other dogs, don't be dragging him away from bigger dogs; he needs to learn and that's exactly what he will do, learn from other dogs' behaviour. Let your pup sniff other dogs. Let people approach him and give him cuddles and stroking. Try not to restrict your dog in any way from all these things.

The key to this period of time is **socialisation.** I actually can't stress this enough. It is absolutely imperative to how your dog learns and how it will hold him in good stead for the rest of his life. **Also, mental stimulation is vital too**, via training. (I will talk about puppy school and training later.) Your dog is naturally inquisitive and a lot more intelligent than people give them credit for. Hide some treats in different places in your lounge, let him sniff them out. It's a natural thing for them to do.

I would also recommend that at this time you begin to leave your puppy alone in the house, just for short periods at a time. Dogs will quickly become totally dependent on you, and separation anxiety, believe me, is an awful thing. He therefore needs to start to learn a little independence too. As your dog gets older, you can leave him alone for slightly longer periods. But I personally would limit this to no more than three hours.

If you're all going to be out of the house all day, please invest in a good local dog walker. A good dog walker will also provide a service of puppy visits. This simply involves them coming into your house to let them out into the garden, and just give them half an hour of company and playtime.

Now is the time for a trip to the vet too. Ask about not only vaccinations but flea and worming treatment. Also get advice from your vet regarding food and nutrition (see later).

Puppy school is an excellent idea at this stage. If money is tight then go online; there are loads and loads of dog training videos you can learn from. If you can afford to then definitely find a good local puppy school. One to one training is pointless at this stage, your dog will get much more out of a group class. Recall and lead training should be at the top of the list, plus basic commands like 'sit' and 'stay'. Any more advanced trick training can follow on after the basics have been mastered.

Don't forget, a good dog trainer isn't training your dog directly, but is training you, the owner, how to train your dog yourself. Keep on practising what you have learnt in puppy school at home. Repetition and positive reinforcement. Your puppy is constantly learning correct behaviour and he not only needs regular exercise but also mental stimulation. Training at home will provide him with this.

One of the unique things about a dog is they are one a few animals in the whole animal kingdom who will look you directly in the eye. This is a great benefit when it comes to training. Your dog will look at you directly; he is wanting to know what you want him to do next, or he may be asking you for something (food, go out for a wee, some playtime). You need to work out what he wants from you too, it's a two-way street. Getting him to look at you whilst you are training him is a great thing, so encourage, reward and reinforce this behaviour.

Your pup will also start teething after a few weeks. If he starts to nibble on your furniture or table leg, don't get cross with him. Buy him some good strong dog toys to chew on instead, and encourage him to use these with reward and reinforcement. If you notice your pup is destroying his toys, then again definitely go for the tougher toys otherwise he may be swallowing and ingesting bits of plastic or foam from inside a soft toy. This won't be good for him and could block his intestines. I don't like to name drop but Kong are an excellent brand of hard toys, some of which you can stuff with dog treats to keep him occupied.

You may also think after a while your dog doesn't need to be put in the cage or pen at night. That's fine but leave it there and leave it open anyway. This space will have become his safety net and he can choose to go in and out of this area at will. He might not want to be bothered and go for a little nap, so let him do this. He will tell you when he wants something, by coming back out of his pen.

6. Routine

Your dog will feel more at home if you can put some kind of routine in place. They do like to have a routine so set aside regular times for walking, playing, training, etc.

Also make sure he is fed at regular times.

Walked at regular times.

Regular play time with training games for mental stimulation.

Even a regular bedtime walk round the block or trip to the garden.

However, also add other less regular aspects into his life. If you can continue with dog training after the puppy school has finished then definitely do so. Once a week is fine. There are all sorts of training classes he can attend, from more advanced learning of commands, to trick training, agility training and more.

Again, if you can't afford to keep training lessons up, get on the Internet and look for things you would like him to learn, like playing dead, opening doors, commando crawling, etcetera. Whatever you fancy.

Add these into his daily routine and once he has mastered something move onto another trick training game.

Perhaps try a dog 'sport' once a week and add this into his routine. My personal favourite is a sport called Flyball. Look it up. It's fantastic fun. You might want to consider entering into Flyball or agility competitions, they love it.

Try not to take it too seriously if your dog doesn't win… it's the taking part that counts!

It's all about playtime, he will enjoy it so much and love you for taking the time to let him participate.

7. Nutrition and Dental Care

Now I like to think I have good knowledge in general dog care, but I'm certainly not a vet or a nutritional expert.

So please take advice from your vet.

What I would say, however, to give you a guideline are the following little tips.

When your dog is still a puppy, he will need three meals a day. Small but often is the key during this period. Your puppy will grow faster than you could imagine, so he needs regular nutrition to feed his energy levels and his brain. Ask your vet when you should decrease his meals to just twice a day.

Never go down to just one feeding a day; your dog will need two meals a day throughout his life in order to sustain his development and energy levels.

As to the brand of food, well I'm not going to advise you on this, as different breeds may require different brands. Ask your vet, they are the experts. However, please do research into dog food. A few of the leading brands (no names mentioned) are not as good as you might think. They can contain a lot of taste enhancers like oils, fats and sugars. The meat content they claim on the packets are only just on the legal requirements by legislation. And the vegetable content can be just as low. These foods are often best sellers, so be aware and research the options available on the market. Your dog may love the taste of them but it does not mean it is a good balanced diet for him.

Do not walk your dog immediately after feeding them. Leave it a good forty-five minutes. It can cause real problems in their stomach and can lead to fatalities.

Always leave plenty of water for him. Check his water bowls on a very regular basis. They drink a lot and need to remain hydrated at all times. In addition, please don't make the mistake of not leaving water out for them at night time. Some people think it will help to avoid accidents in the night. If you woke in the night dying of thrust, you would go and get yourself a drink of water, so don't deprive your dog of the hydration he needs.

A little extra tip on this. If your dog doesn't seem to be drinking much fresh water, and prefers a good muddy puddle, then try this. Put a tiny drop of milk into his water bowl, let him watch you do it. It sends the water cloudy and he now thinks it's an extra special bowl of water. It's always worked for me! However, not much milk please, just enough to change the colour of the water. Too much dairy product is not good for your dog.

Dental care is important. Once your puppy has done teething and his adult teeth have grown through, it's the same as us humans. You can't just grow another set of teeth. You therefore need to look after your dog's oral hygiene. There are specialist dog toothpastes and toothbrushes available. Again, please ask your vet for advice. I would try to brush them twice a week at least.

I personally also highly recommend denture sticks for your dog. Give it to him as a night time treat on a daily basis, it helps to keep his teeth clean and his breath fresher too.

There are also supplements available for your dog's health that you can add to a meal. Some breeds, for example, suffer from poor joints later in life, so you can add joint supplements to his food from an early age. Fish supplements are also good. I know I'm saying this a lot, but please check with your vet again!

My dog, Ollie, has a combination of dry and wet food each meal. The dry food is fine, but can you imagine eating that twice a day for your whole life and nothing else. By adding a wet pouch into the dried food, you can give him more variety and flavours, and a lot of the wet foods also have vegetables mixed in too.

If your dog is suffering from diarrhoea a great cure is boiled plain rice with boiled chicken. They love it and it helps to settle their tummy, but again (you've guessed it) check with your vet!

Also bear in mind as your dog ages you may need to switch to a different food. Puppy food is different from adult dog food, for example.

I will now give you a quick top ten list of things to never feed your dog. For different reasons these can actually poison your dog and in extreme circumstance it can result in fatality, so please do take note of this. This list isn't exclusive so make sure you know what to avoid. Some of the things on this list may surprise you.

1. Chocolate
2. Grapes
3. Raisins
4. Milk, ice cream, eggs, cheese
5. Salty foods like crisps or popcorn
6. High fat meats like bacon, ham or meat trimmings
7. Garlic and onions
8. Any raw chicken
9. Sweets, candy, chewing gum or other highly sugared foods
10. Avocado

I know, it is surprising, isn't it? If your dog decides he likes vegetables, like a raw carrot, then great. Use these as training treats rather than traditional dog treats.

Another weird one. Ice cubes on a hot day. You might think this is a good way to cool your dog down when he's hot and panting. It will have the reverse effect. Your dog's system will think something extremely cold has just entered, and so it will counter act this by heating your dog up even more, resulting in catastrophe.

If you find your dog is particularly greedy, and literally inhales his food, you can buy dog bowls that have compartments running through them to slow your dog down when eating. They work really well.

Do not **(ever)** feed your dog from your own plate. It may be that you are giving something harmful to him (for example a lot of human food is very salty) and in addition it will only encourage your dog to beg.

Finally, never ever let your dog get overweight. They are just like us in many ways and it can lead to heart conditions and more.

8. Twilight Years

As your dog gets older, his needs will change and he will begin to slow down a little.

However, there is no need to change anything really but rather just make some small adjustments (unless his health becomes very poor).

So, watch out for signs of ageing but stick to the routine, just make some subtle changes. Good signs to look out for are lack of appetite, less water consumption, he may lose some hearing and can even develop poorer eyesight (just like us humans again). Any changes you may notice should prompt a visit to the vets, it maybe he is in pain.

Make the walks a little shorter, but don't just stop exercising completely. He will let you know when he's had enough and wants to go home. Muscle mass is the main driver of a dog's metabolism so if they lose muscle mass they can develop 'frailty syndrome' which can accelerate ageing.

Give him playtime if he is still interested. And why stop teaching him new words or new tricks? Whoever said 'you can't teach an old dog new tricks', what absolute rubbish. He may need mental stimulation even more now as he can't exercise as much.

If your dog becomes arthritic you can buy levitated dog bowls so he doesn't have to bend down to feed. And of course, there is medication available to him for all kinds of illnesses. This is why you must keep up regular health check-up at your vets, including more frequent blood tests to check for signs of poor kidney or liver function.

Perhaps consider getting an orthopaedic bed as a good restful sleep can help improve mobility and reduce stiffness. If this is too expensive then you can just put more blankets or old towels around and in his bed area.

If he develops poor mobility problems then a support sling will also help. It should have a handle on the back which allows you to help him get into the car, climb stairs, etcetera. Even a ramp for the car would be a good idea too.

If you have wooden floors also think about putting some carpet or rugs down to prevent him from slipping and doing further injury.

Check with your vet regarding his nutrition, you may also need to change his diet and use more supplements.

If he needs to take regular pills, putting them inside a piece of ham is always a winner to make sure he swallows the medication down.

So, keep your eyes out for any signs, and keep giving him the love, affection and cuddles he needs. Don't just start to ignore him because he's not the dog he used to be.

See my final chapter for what your dog really wants from you throughout his life.

9. Dog Theft

I added this chapter in at the eleventh hour and the final draft. I felt it important to add in what are the depressing but truthful facts about owning a dog today.

I am a member of many dog-related social groups that involve general facts and questions from other members about their own dogs. Sadly, it seems that every other message is reporting a stolen dog. It's shameful and these terrible people should be tracked down and punished.

The truth is that in just the last twelve months dog thefts have increased by a staggering 170%. Dogs have become more fashionable, and therefore more expensive, especially during the Covid-19 lockdown. All types, ages, breeds, shapes and sizes, male or female, are being stolen in alarming numbers. This is largely to sell on quickly at a highly reduced rate for some quick cash, or it could be for breeding purposes. Even more sinister, they are used as bait to train fighting dogs.

Unfortunately, the police do not have to investigate a dog theft and if the breed is inexpensive then it falls under the lowest category of theft and rarely leads to a custodial sentence. As little as one percent of cases make it to court. Campaigners have been organising online petitions to try to increase the category of dog thefts, here is hoping. More recently new legislation has been introduced to make dog microchipping compulsory, so things are moving in the right direction.

My tips to keep your dog safe from these criminal monsters are as follows:

1. Microchipping. Make sure your dog has one and its details are up to date with your vets (if you have moved to a new house for example). Reputable breeders will have had the pups microchipped before selling them on. Always check. Most dogs that do get returned have a microchip.

2. Always have a collar and tag. Do not put your dog's name on the tag, only your name and number. A dog is more likely to go off with someone if they know its name.

3. Never ever leave your dog unattended. I hear so often of people who have tied their dog up outside a shop whilst 'nipping in' for a pint of milk.

4. Never leave your dog in the car (you should not anyway, especially in the summer).

5. Make sure your garden is fully secure. And make sure you can see your dog from inside if you have let them out in the garden.

6. Take updated photos of your dog from all angles (you probably do anyway!) and photograph any distinguishing features.

7. Make sure your dog's recall is excellent. It should be one of the first things you teach them anyway.

8. Be vigilant whilst out walking your dog. It is often the case that your dog has been targeted by criminal groups for the value. Try not to get distracted by someone making conversation, it could be a trap.

9. Be suspicious of unknown cars parked up around your house. Make a note of the vehicle registration, or if it is safe take a photo. Your house might be being scoped out by thieves.

10. If your dog does get stolen, phone the police and jump straight onto your social media platforms. Post pictures of your dog and get all your friends to share the post. Do this straight away. Also use the site DogLost and do the same.

11. Be suspicious of people advertising dogs for much cheaper than the breed will usually cost. The chances are that dog or dogs are stolen. Report them.

Mostly just be vigilant, be suspicious and never take your eyes off your dog when outside. It's common sense but people can become complacent and then it's too late.

10. Love and Loyalty for Life

Basically, you should always treat your dog like you might treat your own child. After all, a dog is an extension of your family, or it might be just the two of you. Either way it all comes down to the following.

Your dog needs love, affection, learning, play time, socialisation, mental stimulation, exercise and good food. Never shout at your dog when he wrongs you, and never ever hit your dog in anger.

If you follow my basic guidelines, then you should not go too far wrong. Your dog wants to please you.

If you treat him with the respect and love he deserves, then he will give it back to you ten times over. Remember dogs are for life.

Good luck and enjoy your dog, he will be your best friend ever.

Always happy to see me, with wagging tail and kisses
When I come home, I therefore know it's me he misses.

If I've had a bad day, he doesn't ask me why
He just cuddles closer to me, especially if I cry.

When I'm feeling blue, I like to pull him tighter
He doesn't mind, as he knows, it makes me feel much brighter.

Our friendship is so strong, I can feel it in my heart
And that is why I never ever, want us to be apart.

That's because I love him, and give him fun and play
I always make sure this happens every single day.

We walk together all the time, even rain or shine
He loves me back for it, because he knows he's mine.

He gives back his love and loyalty, right until the end
And he always knows, that he is my very best friend.

THE END